In Defense of the Pastor
and
Other Tales of Disaster

Paul Palumbo

I found myself far from you
in the land of false images.

St. Augustine
The Confessions

Contents

In Defense of the Pastor

Introduction

The simple truth is this: all pastors have stories about ourselves that are too embarrassing to share, stories about our foolishness and folly in ministry. We try to forget them, push them aside, or tell counter-stories to reassure ourselves that we are not so bad, after all.

It doesn't work. The stories of our disasters remain a part of us and have a huge effect on our lives as pastors. If you are like me, the memory of past mistakes leads you to go to great lengths to avoid making them again. We know we don't want to go through that angst again, so, slowly and subtly, protecting ourselves from mistakes becomes the underlying focus of our pastoral lives. How constantly do we work to protect ourselves from even the appearance of a misstep? Here is a quick test. A parishioner comes to you with a serious look on his or her face and says, "Pastor, I need to speak to you." What is the very first thing that comes to your mind? Is it a quick inventory of past interactions, issues that might come up, things you might have said to offend this person? In short, is your first response, "What have I done that I might now have to defend?"

If this is anything like your honest first response, then you know what it is like to do ministry out of, it's okay to say it, vanity. Vanity in our culture is kind of a "silly" sin--"Oh, he's so vain!" connotes someone who looks in the mirror every chance he gets.

But the nearly instinctive move to defend oneself is the clear sign of this insidious sin--and it gives clear meaning to the ancient words, "Vanity of vanities, all is vanity!"

It seems quite natural to want to protect ourselves from the shame of being wrong, hurtful to others, mistaken. But the natural response is untenable. There are too many encounters with too many people to guard ourselves from the mistakes of ministry. We will mess up again. And when we do, the shame and the angst will intensify and call us to even greater efforts of protection. Does vanity never cease?

You would think that making mistakes was not that big a deal. And on the surface, you would be correct. Of course we mess up, misread, misunderstand. Most often, we apologize, shake it off and carry on. But there are some events that set us on a downward spiral of shame and self-loathing. How is it, then, that some of our mistakes are no big deal while others put us in an existential crisis? I think the great screw-ups of our ministry are those that call into doubt the images we have of ourselves as pastors.

Over the years, I have accumulated a host of characteristics, some of which are helpful to pastoral ministry. Being a good preacher or a calm presence in a crisis will get you a long way as a pastor. However, these characteristics begin to take on a life of their own. Subtly and slowly, they change from being something I *do* to something I *am*. As soon as that transition is made, and it sure does sneak up on a person, then whatever threatens them threatens me. For example, if I deliver a less than stellar sermon, one that ought to evoke from me something like "That was not a very good sermon," what I sometimes find myself *feeling* is self-loathing. "I am a pathetic preacher! Why am I even doing this?" Every poor sermon becomes an attack on my self-image.

Of course, it doesn't last long. You get over it quickly and move on. Better sermon next week, right? Of course you get over it. And if it were just one sermon once in a while, that would be fine. But what if we have, not a couple characteristics that get internalized, but thousands of them? And every one of them insists upon the kind of defense that fear and self-preservation demand? Now we are talking about our lives being overrun with the daily maintenance of our self-images. Every pastoral act, every interaction is fraught with danger. Our lives, supposedly given over to Christ and loving His people, can become a minefield through which we walk gingerly so as not to blow up any of the well-cultivated images we have of ourselves. This is what happened to me as I went about my work, and what sometimes still sneaks up on me. It is embarrassing to admit how much energy I have spent on maintaining images. It is exhausting.

I am told that pastors are often uninspired and frustrated, tired and burned out. I contend that the source of this weariness is not the work itself, but the hidden internal struggle of vanity I am describing. My guess is that it afflicts most of us, and that most of the time, we are not fully aware of it. And if we are aware of it, it seems so immature that it's hard to admit that a person in our position would be caught up in such foolishness. So we either do not see it, or we begin to see, and it is so embarrassing that we want like crazy to hide it! Of course, this is a disaster because now we heap shame on top of vanity! Now, *for sure* we don't want anybody to know about it!

This is an insidious dynamic. Even as it drives us to the brink of exhaustion, our vanity remains *hidden*. We blame the 'stress of the job' and draw away from the edge. We take a vacation or a sabbatical. We commit to working more efficiently or more carefully, anything to get over it. I know. I did all those things. Unfortunately, these survival strategies only serve to maintain the very images that are killing us. The problem is not that we are driven to the brink. The problem is that we think we are supposed to survive the trip! We are not supposed to survive. Not if we take the story of Jesus seriously, anyway. Die, already, and be done with it. Die to the images we have of ourselves, to the good we have done or have not done, to the success we have or thought we should have. Jesus calls us from the other side of the grave. The only way to follow, the only way to be free of the anxiety, the self-judging, and the exhaustion, is to let those images die. Of course, first we have to acknowledge that we have such images, depend upon them and protect them. In short, we must confess our vanity.

For me, the way out is by taking St. Paul at his word, "...For you have died and your life is hidden with Christ in God." Dying to one's self--to the images to which we attempt to conform--is a fundamental tenet of the Christian faith. But to take these words seriously, I want to say *literally*, has led me to feel, in my bones, something of what St. Paul meant. This is how I have heard it echoing in my ears and heart for the past few years: 'Listen! *You are already dead!* That 'self' you are so busy maintaining and defending? It's nothing but a corpse. It has been put to death in baptism. Your life is now and forever hidden with Christ in God.' Over the past few years, letting go, dying, has been the theme of my pastoral life and the object of my reflections.

So here are some stories that exposed my vanity and, paradoxically, led me to a place of freedom. Stories of true pastoral disasters that called into question my self-worth and vocation, and stories of a dawning realization that dying can be a completely liberating experience. There are also some tales of living deeply in the freedom of the crucified and risen Christ. They are all mixed in because the realization of dying in Christ is not a straightforward experience. The old Self does not die easily and I continue to slip back into old images and create new ones. What delights me, though, is that, when I catch the old Self demanding to be protected and me rising up in defense, I often end up laughing and letting it go with a simple reminder. 'Who am I trying to impress? I'm dead, for God's sake!'

May this book lead you to your own stories and to the truth that you, too, are dead. There is nothing to defend. Your life is hidden with Christ in God.

Fear and Shame

You want to make a good impression at college? Try having a grand mal seizure on the very first day of your freshman year, in the middle of a dorm-hall meeting. I'd never had a seizure before in my life and out of the blue, it hit me. Of course, I knew nothing about it. I was completely checked out, until several hours later when I came to in the hospital. It took a day or two to recover and then it was back to school where I was now famous for something of which I had no recollection. Naturally, the guys on the floor were sensitive to my plight. They just called me 'Seizure Boy' and fell to the ground shaking when they saw me coming down the hall.

In those first two weeks or so, I wasn't sure which was worse, the embarrassment of having had a seizure in front of everybody or the fear that I would have another. Who knew why it had happened or when it might happen again? And who knew what audience there might be?

Years later, as I happened to be driving on the highway, for some reason I started thinking about seizures and how they give no warning when they come. Mind you, I had not had a seizure in almost *thirty years.* Nevertheless, the more I thought about seizures and the possibility of having one out of the blue, the more my heart started pounding. *What if I have a seizure right here as I'm driving on the highway? What if they start coming back?* I got light-headed just thinking about it and was fighting to keep my attention on driving. Finally, I pulled over to the side of the road, threw the car into park and put my head down. I was not having a seizure, but there I was on the side of the road, physically unable to continue until the anxiety passed. Naturally, I told no one of this ridiculous episode.

It is the same with my interior life. What if I mess up? What if people see what a frightened person I really am? What if people found out that I am not really very smart, or nice, or compassionate or whatever? At times, the fear of being exposed can lock me up and keep me from being present in the moment, unable to risk being myself. Under the spell of such fear, I stop whatever I might otherwise be doing, and try to find a safe space to park. Don't take the risk of preaching truthfully and personally, don't risk further personal interaction with anyone, don't even risk truthfulness before God in prayer!

I went for a day retreat a while back to spend time in prayer, with some colleagues. I was still grieving the suicide of my best friend, my father-in-law had had a life-threatening stroke, our children were chronically sick living in a musty house, and I thought a day of prayer would be good for me. We arrived at the retreat house where we spent time alternating between solitary prayer and community sharing. Eager as I was to try out the rhythm of the retreat, I found the time of solitude unbearable due to fear. What was I afraid of? For one thing, I was afraid of dying. My friend's death was so recent and so raw that I couldn't face it. Sitting alone, memories of my friend and thoughts of mortality raced through my mind. My heart pounded, trying to keep up. Instead of praying, I spent the time taking my pulse: seventy-five, eighty, ninety beats a minute. It was agony to sit alone for the agreed upon half hour, all the while thinking I was going to die before ever reuniting with the others. The moment I heard the chime signaling that we were to reunite, I was out of my chair and sprinting down the hallway to the commons area. I did not drop dead, after all! Just before turning the corner, however, I slowed down to a dignified stroll, entering the presence of others as cool as could be. Arriving in the commons area, my relief at not dying immediately turned into shame over having been afraid. There was no way I was going to let my colleagues know what had happened in my time alone. I was supposed to be a pastor and I was afraid of being alone with God?

So I sat with the others, listening to them speak about their experience, what had come, how they had relaxed into the silence. Too embarrassed to share my fear, I now found myself eager to get away from my colleagues and my shame. Fear in solitude was better than shame before others, I reckoned. Once back in my room alone, however, I couldn't wait to be reunited. Bouncing from fear to shame all day, the "retreat" that I had hoped for became an insidious, embarrassing endurance contest. Afraid to be alone with God, ashamed to talk about that fear with anyone, I did the logical thing: I swore off prayer retreats.

Fear and shame form a hellish combination. It may not be as blatant or intense as my 'retreat' experience, but I carry a lot of anxiety just below the surface, anxiety of not accomplishing great things, or of doing small things badly. Fear that people will recognize just how selfish, insecure, unfaithful, insensitive, unloving, dispassionate and cynical I can get. There have been times when I have second-guessed every sermon, every interaction, each word that came from my mouth. And that's only the half of it, because then shame would swallow me up. *How can you be so insecure? What an egomaniac! Don't let this out!*

In those times, it seemed there was nothing I could do to get out of the cycle. Afraid and ashamed, unable or unwilling to move in any direction, the best I could do was to find a safe place and put my head down, parked on the side of the road.

"Yes, Ma'am"

"Now, he is not a civil man, Pastor, so you just have to leave him to me."

"Fine with me!" I said enthusiastically.

Jean Winters was in charge of the grounds at our church, and she was giving me warning about Mr. Branson, the ornery old cuss whom she had hired to cut the lawn. I was new as the pastor of the church and I surely did not want to do anything to offend the guy, lest I end up having to cut the grass myself. I kept my distance from him, not even saying 'Good morning' when I saw him at work every other Saturday. However, one Saturday morning, I pulled up to the church and found Mr. Branson cutting the grass on an off week. We had communion every other week, and it was on communion weekends that he would cut the grass. But this was not a communion weekend. So now I'm thinking really hard because if it's not a communion Sunday, and the grass is being mowed, there must be something special going on that I had missed. A baptism? Anniversary? Special guests? How could I, the pastor, have missed the news about something special going on in church? Instead of going inside and making a phone call like a mature person would, my confusion got to me and I panicked. I asked the grass cutter if he was told that there was something special going on that he needed to cut the grass.

"I know my goddamned schedule!" he shouted, "I don't need nobody telling me what my schedule is!"

Ah! Not a civil man. I muttered my apologies and headed inside, where my shame immediately began to grow. Not only did I apparently not know the church schedule as well as the grass cutter, now I was ashamed that he was so derisive with me, that I let him be that way and that it was *I* who apologized! The more I thought about it, the more my shame turned to anger. Before I knew it, I had conjured up a strong brew of righteous indignation. Nobody needed to act like that. It was a simple question, a legitimate question, and who the hell does he think he is, anyway, talking to the *Pastor* that way?

As I left the building a short while later, Mr. Branson was out in the parking lot talking with the president of the congregation who happened to have wandered by. I heard him telling his side of the story, that he didn't want any trouble, that he knew his schedule. At this, I exploded, matching his arrogance with my own.

"You certainly will have trouble if you jump in my face like that over a simple question!"

"I don't have to answer to you! I know my goddamn schedule!"

"Maybe you do, but there is no way you are going to work here if you can't field one simple goddamned question!"

The shouting match was on! A crowd gathered as we went face to face right there on the steps of the church. I had not been in a fight in a long time, but there was no way I was going to let that man treat me that way. I was the pastor, goddammit! If he wanted to fight about it, great.

No punches were thrown, thank God, and cooler heads prevailed. I got into my car and drove away from there. No sooner had I pulled out, however, than I began to see the foolishness of my actions. What non-sense to have the pastor in a shouting match on the front steps of the church where the Prince of Peace is worshiped, demanding respect simply for being there. Oh yeah, and how about a young white man publicly threatening the job of an old black man in the middle of the community where that man has lived most of his life? What insecure arrogance! I guess everybody in that crowd saw me for the *kid* I was. Trying to have some authority…over the guy who cuts the grass! The entire encounter, from the moment I pulled up into the parking lot to the moment I got back into my car was an embarrassing disaster. After this, I would never be accepted or respected. I had ruined whatever chance I had at being a good pastor here. All that day, self-loathing gnawed at me. I tried to tell myself that it was not *that bad*, that it was okay to defend myself, but I remained unconvinced and my stomach was in knots all day.

The next morning, still feeling like I had ruined everything, I knew what I had to do. After church I found Jean and asked her to walk outside with me.

"Jean," I said, "I think you are going to have an angry grass cutter on your hands."

To which she quickly replied, "Oh, no, darlin', I already took care of him."

'That's what I'm talkin' about,' I thought to my (kid) self. 'That is the kind of property minister you like to have around. Taking care of that disrespectful, grumpy, son of a...'

But she was talking again. "...and now I'm going to take care of *you*."

'Take care of me?' I was thinking.

"Now, sweetheart, you're both men."

She said this in such a way as to make it clear that this one sentence ought to have explained everything, if only I had ears to hear. It reminded me of how Jesus taught. "The kingdom of God is like a pearl," waiting expectantly for his followers to comprehend. And like Jesus' followers who had no idea what he was talking about, so was I with Jean.

She recognized this and went on to explain.

"You're both men. So it's only natural that you are going to get riled up over nothing once in a while. Prideful is all it is."

Jean was naming one of the seven deadly sins, making me completely aware of my participation in it, and doing so in such a genteel manner that I actually smiled in resignation to the truth of it. This kind of pastoral care, you can't teach!

She continued, "But, honey, we didn't call you to take care of the grass, that's my job. We called you to preach and to teach the Bible, to baptize and visit the sick. That's your job. Now, you take care of your job, I'll take care of mine, and I know you are going to do just fine here."

Several responses came rushing through my head as she spoke, all reminiscent of the defense I tried to make for myself the day before. I needed her to know just how disrespectful this man had been, how the pastoral office was at stake, how it was an innocent question in the first place. Inexplicably, however, all I managed to say was, "Yes, Ma'am."

And in that instant, my shame and my defenses literally *evaporated* and I knew I did not have to get Jean to see what I did or why I did it. The gnawing in my gut was gone, replaced by serene joy. All the defenses in the world could not have left me with the peace that submitting to Jean Winters gave me. How foolish my defense was in the face of her clarity and her absolution. It was pure grace that let those words pass

23

from my mouth, "Yes, Ma'am." Two of the most important words I have ever spoken.

Now Available

The instinct to defend myself is so natural and so fast that I often don't even know I am doing it. Or, I do know it and simply live with it. After all, what difference does it make?

It makes all the difference in the world.

When I went away to college, I entered into a world that was much different from the world in which I grew up. The politics were especially strange to me. Issues of social justice and critique of the United States were commonplace at college. In my family, the only time politics was talked about was when my sister's boyfriend would come around to argue with my dad about the Vietnam War or the civil rights movement. These were never really debates, but ever-escalating and unresolvable arguments. I wondered why this knucklehead ever brought it up in the first place.

After a few years in college, I became the knucklehead. Of course, the Vietnam War was over, but there were still plenty of injustices to be angry about. And so I was. For the next twenty years, I became the radical of the family. The good news was that I lived away from home and they did not have to endure my political positions every day. When I visited, however, it was a constant struggle to keep things from degenerating into political shout-downs. It was a struggle we often lost. We are Italian, for God's sake! We are all opinionated people, and inevitably someone would say something that provoked a response. Away we would go, arguing into the night until nothing could redeem the evening. I would go to bed with a pit in my stomach and would swear to do better next time. I suspect that my parents, brothers and sisters could sum up my visits over the years with the motto, "Good to see him, good to see him leave."

Of course, we have all grown up some. But even as a mature adult, I fell into this pattern of dissension with my family. As much as I resolved to hold my tongue, I could not. *I am a person who cares about justice and the poor! It is my duty to challenge, to educate, to agitate my family.* If I did not do it, I would be compromising myself and not living up to my identity.

So the options were to continue to live up to that identity and pester my family, which left me feeling self-righteous but sorrowful, or not saying anything and feeling disappointed in myself for not having the courage to confront my family. This does not make for fun family vacations! Why did I have to continue to bring grief and frustration to people I loved? *Because you are supposed to speak for the voiceless!* Why did I have to have them agree with me on anything? *Because if you can't even get your family to agree with you, how will you convince anyone else?* What if I simply let go of this foolishness and love my family? *You will be a sellout!*

This internal dialogue is exhausting! It goes nowhere, which is the point. I want my images to stay put and be maintained. But it is I who finally must let go. Let the images die. 'Okay, the voiceless will remain voiceless while I am visiting my family!' 'Okay, I probably will never again convince anyone of my position.' 'Okay, I am a sellout who has let go of any notion to change, agitate or challenge my family. Die, already!'

Over the past several years, my visits home have not been marred by the horrible specter of escalating conflict. It was not easy to hear the FOX news version of reality proclaimed as if it were from the mouth of God. I bit my tongue a lot, breathed a lot and eventually I got to the point where I did not feel I would explode if I remained quiet. From there, it was a short step to actually listening more deeply and more compassionately. I began to hear things that I would never have heard before.

My oldest brother, Joe, was telling me about his new job at a high school. Through a series of unexpected events, he was offered a job with the stipulation that he pursue his degree while he worked. So he set out on a new job and a college education.

I heard the story and celebrated his good fortune. We stayed up late into the night. Finally, at 2 in the morning, he told me he had to get some sleep so he could get up and work on a paper for school. We laughed at that! Both of us are too old to be worrying about a paper due for a class!

"What are you writing about?" I asked.

"The war in Iraq, but I am having a really hard time with it."

"Why is that?" I asked, noticing that my stomach was starting to feel tight. It had been such a wonderful evening, I didn't want it to end on a bad note.

"Well, I started out writing a paper in defense of the war. Why it was a good thing to invade Iraq. But the more I worked on it, the more trouble I had with it. This morning I realized that the problem is that I don't think it was a good thing to invade Iraq. So now I have to change the whole thing."

What I thought was, 'Dang! That's a surprise! This is a guy who supported George Bush all the way!' but what I said was, "Hmm."

I did not trust my lips enough to even let them open.

"Yeah, my wife will think I'm crazy, but I can't deny what I think."

"Hmmm."

We departed. Later, I thought about it and realized that I would never have heard that last story if I had not let go of my "family-agitator" identity. In fact, I would have probably inspired my brother to look harder for justification to the war! Instead, we stumbled onto common ground. Normally, I would have considered this a great moral victory. Not that night, though. That night, the great victory was that my brother and I loved each other *differently*. It was pure joy.

Yet I so often miss it. Too busy with the upkeep of my identity, I neglect to live in the present love of God. So much of my life has been spent in upkeep. Parts of my ministry bear witness to the consequences thereof. I am convinced that both the embarrassingly shallow and the profoundly sad screw-ups of my life and ministry begin and end with the relentless upkeep of my self-images. My internal agent keeps trying to make me look good. Of course, the theological and existential point of the Lutheran tradition of which I am a part is that being good is not the point! The love of God does not come to us or through us by our being good. It is a gift. I believe this, I preach it, I may even stand and fall on it, but I rarely experience it. Instead, self-justifying images are created and maintained so that I see myself as the worthy person God wants.

But God does not want people who are *worthy*. God wants people who are *dead*. And not because dying makes me worthy, it simply makes me *available* to be raised from death into a life of freedom. Die, and there is nothing to defend.

I know this. I have experienced it a time or two. But the process of self-justification and image making is insidious. Even now, my inner voice is setting up another image. *Hey! You can be the guy who dies to self-justifying images!*

29

Eyes of Grace

"When did you first know you wanted to be a pastor?"

I have been asked this many times over the years. The question nobody has ever asked me--and the way more interesting one--is, "When was the first time you wanted to *get out of* being a pastor?"

In my case, the answer to both involves encounters with Grace.

It took quite a long time for me to want to be a pastor. I had been serving a church for three years before I *really* wanted to be one. The journey towards embracing my calling began with a conversation in the fellowship hall after my trial sermon at Abiding Savior Lutheran Church. As with every potential candidate, the congregation gathered to hear me preach at a Sunday service. My sermon was completely forgettable, I'm sure, but the people of Abiding Savior were gracious and hospitable. After the service, everyone came to greet Virginia and me and to meet our two little ones, who had come with us. At one point, I was holding my four year old daughter, Maggie, and speaking with a delightful woman of the church. At that time, Maggie was enamored of beads. She had a collection of all kinds, shapes and sizes. It was always the first thing she noticed wherever we went. Well, there I was talking with this woman, whose name, I learned, was Grace. Maggie interrupted us, grabbing my head to turn it so that she could whisper into my ear, "Ooh, Daddy, RED BEADS!"

At this point, Grace tilted her head inquiringly, and I explained. "Maggie loves beads and she is admiring your necklace."

"Oh!" She said, eyes dancing and hands immediately going to the back of her neck. "Where I come from, if someone admires something you have"-- she took the bead necklace from around her own neck and placed it around my little girl's neck--"you give it to them."

Maggie's eyes now danced with Grace's in celebration that those beautiful red beads were now around *her* very own neck! I mumbled a "Thank you," but what was running through my head as I witnessed this simple act of kindness was, 'Please let me come here to be the pastor of this place! Please let me live in a community that does stuff like that!' I am not at all sure that these words did not tumble out of my mouth at that very moment. Whether or not the church needed me, I certainly needed that church; needed to learn to receive and to give, to bear witness to the beauty of a faithful community. I could, for the first time, imagine in that short exchange that this was what my life was for.

I was called to Abiding Savior, and in the course of our life together, I would have ample opportunity to witness, receive and offer such kindness and graciousness. It saddens me still that when, years later, I had occasion to express compassion to Grace, I was not nearly as ready to do so as she had been that morning.

You see, Grace's oldest daughter, Laura, struggled mightily with drug addiction, living from place to place, chasing her habit. She ended up pregnant and Grace committed to raising the child, little Joanna. Laura continued in her addiction and another child was born to her. This child, however, was not going to be raised by her grandparents. She would be given up for adoption. Grace approached me about having the baby baptized before she would be given over to foster care and into the system. I suggested that since the child would be leaving very soon, it would be better not to baptize her into this community but to let her be baptized into the faith community of her adoptive family.

Of course, there was no guarantee that the adoptive parents would care to do so, but the promise that the congregation makes in baptism, to faithfully bring the child to the services of God's house, to teach the Lord's prayer and the Ten Commandments, to place the scriptures in her hands and provide for instruction in the Christian faith, these would not be possible if the child were not among us. That was my thinking. There may even be good reason for it, but even now I feel myself trying to justify my actions. The truth of the matter is that a grandmother who struggled mightily to do what was best for her granddaughter and her family came to the difficult and heart-wrenching decision to let go of this newborn child, and the one thing she most needed was the promise from God spoken and enacted over this child, and I wasn't seeing it. What was I thinking? I was thinking about how important the community is to baptism, how we have lost the sense of baptism *into* a community. I was thinking about being the protector of the integrity of the sacrament! In thinking thus, I failed to speak and enact the very promise of God which the sacrament embodies.

It gets worse, I am sad to say. Yet another child was born, a baby boy. Grandma never approached me about baptizing this child. There was no discussion of baptizing this baby who was also headed for adoption.

But the child never made it to adoption. He died in a car crash before he was three months old...unbaptized.

I know that baptism is not about getting into heaven, it is not a hedge against the condemnation of God. God's mercy is far greater than that. But I also know that the promise embodied in baptism is so powerful that any doubt or fear for a beloved one's soul can be overcome. God's promise does that. Not as a ticket into heaven, but as a spoken promise that whatever comes in the future, our loving God will meet us there. The tragedy is that Grace never got to hear that promise spoken over her grandbabies. One left her home, and the other died before anyone, before I, her pastor, spoke that promise over them.

I knew what I had to do. I went to visit Grace. The entire way there I tried to figure out what I was supposed to do when I arrived. How could I give comfort to this grieving woman when I knew I had been a part of that grief? I found her with a friend, distractedly moving about the house from room to room. She greeted me, but kept up her flight. Chasing her about the house, I gave my condolences about the baby, but that did not seem to relieve my burden, which now, I am ashamed to admit, became my main focus. Grace did not bring up the fact that the child was not baptized, but in my guilt and self-justifying stupor, I had to. I had to tell her something, anything, so I told her that in the ancient church, for those who died before they were baptized, death itself was considered to be their baptism.

There! I had taken my best shot at comforting Grace and relieving my guilt.

With eyes on fire, she whipped around at me and said, "You know, some day that might give me some comfort, but right now, frankly, I don't see how!"

Of course, she couldn't see how. It was never intended to give her comfort. It was meant to give *me* comfort. It was meant to justify my position and to address the anxiety I felt for the terrible part I played in this sad drama. When her eyes shone on my cowardice, my face instantly grew hot with embarrassment and all I wanted to do was to get out from the searing light of her glare, out of her house and out of ministry. What else could I do when the shameful truth was made so clear? I wasn't in it to accompany Grace in her suffering, I was in this to save myself from the pain of having gotten it all so wrong, from the shame of intentionally choosing to justify myself rather than console a grandmother who mourned.

Ministry had gone horribly wrong. How could my work ever come to such a graceless dead end? How could there be any way forward in ministry? There was none. I left that house and lived the best I could with the weight of my shame. For months, every proclamation I made rang hollow, every conversation I entered into was marred by fear that the person with whom I was speaking knew all about my colossal failure. Ashamed and afraid of being further exposed, I all but disqualified myself from the office of pastor. I faded into the background as much as I could. No bold sermons, no strong pastoral leadership, no risks. I no longer thought that this was what my life was for and for the first time since I had embraced my calling to be a pastor, I wanted out.

In Defense of the Pastor

"Everything is fine here, Pastor, no problems. Oh, and I fired the musician."

I had just returned from a week of vacation. My mind was relaxed and ready to get back into the swing of things, and this is what I come home to?

"You *what*?"

"Yeah, I fired him. He was late again on Sunday morning and was ugly with the choir on Wednesday night. He won't stop drinking, Pastor, so I fired him. It had to be done."

It was true. Our musician had been given lots of chances, plenty of support and was still unable to perform his duties. In the end, he lost his job and we lost a very fine musician. It was sad all the way around.

Deep down, though, I felt a great sense of relief. In fact, this was a great outcome for me. It was inevitable that the church had to fire the guy. As difficult and ugly as it would be, the musician clearly was not working out. I knew it, but I certainly didn't want to deal with it. I tried to convince myself that this was an issue of compassion and commitment. The church should reflect the God it believes in, right? We are to be gracious and merciful to one another, just as God is with us. How could we, the church, fire someone who was struggling? Shouldn't we be rallying beside this man and helping him get through his addiction?

This was what I told myself and sure, there is some truth in it. The church is called to compassion. But my motives had little to do with compassion. They had to do with perpetuating my reputation as a compassionate person, who saw the best in others, tolerated their weaknesses and hoped for the best to emerge from them. That was the real issue. As much friction as was being generated between the musician and the choir, I was unwilling to step out of the role of the "caring pastor." Of course, the bind there was that I had to work doubly hard to convince the choir that I was also caring for them! I encouraged them to be tolerant, and they were. I extolled the virtues of being patient, and they were. Finally, though, enough was enough. I would have continued tolerating bad behavior forever and before you know it, there would have been no more choir members. So the president did what was needed. The musician was dismissed. The beauty of it was I steered clear of the whole mess. It was the president who had done the deed. He was the bad guy. Perfect! My self-image intact, I *was* ready to get back into the swing of things! In other words, I could continue to maintain the illusion of my life.

Years later, there was another firing, this time of a young man who wasn't working out at the Community

Center. He appealed to me, as an officer of the board of directors, to hear his side of the story and the rest of the board had agreed. Sitting in my office he tried to convince me that the board was wrong, even immoral to dismiss him. When I remained unmoved, he made the case that my participation in his dismissal was also immoral, un-Christian.

"I am not a Christian, but what you are doing is not what Jesus would do! What kind of a Christian are you, anyway, and a pastor, too?"

My heart gave that familiar wrench as it does whenever my sense of self is attacked. I felt shame, as if simply by speaking, he had made his accusation true. I *felt* un-Christian, unmerciful. How could I hold my position that he was rightly fired and yet avoid the guilt of being a lousy ambassador of Jesus?

In the face of threat to my self-image, fear drives me to defend myself. It happens all the time and now, sitting in my office, it was happening again. Quickly, I made an assessment of how to handle the situation. Fortunately this was familiar territory. I had my response ready. 'You have been sitting here telling me how you are not a Christian and now you accuse me of not living up to what you don't even believe?' That would do it! Or, I could simply muscle through the feelings of guilt and process them later. I've certainly done that before.

But that day I chose neither. Perhaps because it was a week or two before Christmas, but for some reason 'Go Tell it on the Mountain' popped into my head, specifically, the line "and if I am a Christian, I am the least of all." I asked myself, "What am I defending? Who am I trying to be?" In an instant, all the anxiety and shame evaporated, replaced by, of all things, playfulness! Maybe that is the proper response when you finally wake up, I don't know. What I do know is that all the anxiety and all the energy expended to defend myself was transformed into lightness. I knew exactly what to say.

"What kind of Christian am I? Not a very good one. In fact, most of the time, I suck at it! But you are still fired."

His response was as surprising as my own.

"I don't think I have ever heard anybody say anything like that before." And he started to laugh.

He tried another run or two at me, but his heart was no longer in it. I guess we both realized that there was nowhere else to go. Guilt, humiliation, manipulation; there was no room for them anymore. He left my office scratching his head. I stayed put, basking in the giddiness of this new experience. Relieved of the notion of the good pastor, the model Christian, the nice guy, the whatever, there was no shame, no guilt, no anger. If I am a Christian, I am the least of all! No need to fabricate, promote or enhance false notions. Jesus is quite clear what kind of Christian I am; most of the time I suck at it.

Landing

A good way to tell about Hearthside is to tell a more recent story. I now live in Washington State. I took our youth group to Seattle to get a tour of the city with Verlon Brown. Verlon has a street ministry with heroin addicts and his tours are not on the <u>101 Things to Do in Seattle</u> brochure. But if you want to see the Gospel in the brokenness of human life, Verlon is your man. At one stop on the tour, we were on the street listening to a young woman describe her ministry feeding the homeless population. As we gathered around, a man from the streets sidled up next to my son and slapped him on the chest to get his attention. I quietly made my way over to see what was going on and heard the man say, "Hey, you from North Carolina? Or do you just like the UNC cap?"

Sam was wearing the omnipresent University of North Carolina baseball cap.

"Yeah, we are from North Carolina."

"Where in North Carolina?"

"Durham."

"Get the fuck outta here! I'm from Durham."

"Oh, cool!"

"Where in Durham?"

At this point Sam was a little unsure so he nodded at me.

"You know North Carolina Central and Old Alston Avenue?" I asked.

"Sure do!"

"We lived down Old Alston Avenue. You know Unity Village?"

"Get the fuck outta here! You lived in Unity Village?"

"Well, right near there. You know Hearthside?"

"Get the fuck *outta* here! I *know* you didn't live in no Hearthside!"

"Right next door. I was pastor there for ten years."

"Damn! You are one crazy white man! I live on the streets of Seattle and I wouldn't even *think* of living near no Hearthside."

We lived 100 yards from Hearthside. For most of our first two years there, I looked out the back window of our house and thought more or less the same thing as my Seattle friend. "I wouldn't even think of going into no Hearthside." The Haitians were trying to gain ground there against local Durham drug gangs and every other night there was one confrontation or another. Shootings and knife fights were commonplace. However bad it was, the really heavy drug dealing and violence ended at the end of Hearthside Street. Only on rare occasions would these things spill out into the rest of the neighborhood, but mostly it stayed in Hearthside itself. So if somebody wanted to avoid it, they would simply not enter into Hearthside. What kept all the hostility and violence inside that small housing project, I do not know. What kept me *out*, I know without question: fear, not only of physical harm, but of being mocked and made fun of. I could not imagine myself walking past the gatherings of young men and having a conversation with them. How would I relate to them?

From the back window of our new house, I could see around the trees to Hearthside. The image out that window is still vivid in my mind because I stood there often, taking in the view while I had a short conversation with God about ministry to my neighbors.

God: "Whenever you're ready."

Me: "No way."

I wasn't going there, but my resistance did not stop Hearthside from coming to me. To us, I should say. It happened when we sent Maggie, our firstborn, to the neighborhood elementary school. It did not take long for her to begin inviting her school friends over to play. Once they did, they constantly found their way to our home and into the back yard. It was not at all unusual for us to look out back to find fifteen kids running around, playing on the swings or climbing on the jungle gym. Maggie and Sam were not always keen to have that many kids around, and we tried to keep some semblance of privacy, but our hearts were not in keeping children away. It was clear that this was a safe place for kids from Hearthside to be. Typically, one child who was a regular visitor brought another who became a regular and the numbers increased steadily. Most of the kids made themselves right at home. Virginia put out juice and cups for them and we monitored from the window as each new child arrived and the backyard stayed full.

One child, however, was not so comfortable with this new place. Rodney, as we had known from school, was often rough and had a quick temper. When he first arrived, we were not sure what would happen, so we watched more carefully than usual. Rodney surprised us by staying aloof, not engaging the other kids. He stayed close to the back door, away from the action in the yard. Poking my head out the sliding glass door, I asked him if he needed anything.

"No, I'm just lookin'."

"Okay," I said, "you let me know if I can help you with anything."

Rodney looked up at me then and said, "Where do you go when the shooting starts?"

"I'm sorry, what was that?"

"Where do you go when the shooting starts?"

Lord, have mercy.

"Well, Rodney, where do you go in your house when the shooting starts?"

"I get straight under the bed."

"Well, come with me," I said, and we walked to the bedroom where I opened the door and pointed to the bed. "If shooting starts, you come and get under the bed. I will meet you here."

"All right, then."

And with that pressing issue resolved, off he went to join the rest of the kids in the backyard.

God: "Anytime you're ready."

Me: "No way! Where *do* you go when the shooting starts?"

But with the kids arriving at our home, it was only a matter of time before they began inviting me to come and meet their families. I said, "Not today" so often that even the kids started wondering what the problem was. I had to go back to my window for one more conversation with God.

God: "Are you ready yet? You now have an entourage to escort you."

Me: "Okay, okay, but if I have to go over there, I'm wearing my collar. I don't want anybody thinking some white man got lost and wandered into the wrong place. If they shoot me, I want them to know they are shooting a priest!"

God: "Wear what you want. I care what you wear?"

So, on a Saturday afternoon, when the kids were done playing in our yard, they asked, as usual, if I would come and meet their families. Dressed in my clerical collar (how silly it seems, but it sure gave me some comfort!), off I went with a dozen kids to enter Hearthside for the very first time. Surrounded by the kids, I was fairly sure I was safe from physical harm, but they could not protect me from the looks I got from the young men hanging out on the street. I did not know then what was on their minds, though I knew it was not hospitality. Over the years, as I got to know some of the men in the neighborhood, I have heard their memories of my arrival into Hearthside. They were suspicious and resentful of me being there. I got the message very clearly, but I had made the commitment and now I had to carry it out. Thankfully, the kids all wanted to introduce me to their mothers. As it happened, the first several mothers turned out to be grandmothers who were raising their grandkids. I stood outside as the kids announced my presence, then I stepped into the apartment. To this day, I am thankful for those church-going grandmothers! They were cordial, not warm but cordial, and they gave me the opportunity to find some common ground.

"Oh, you're a pastor?"

"Yes, ma'am, at the Lutheran Church down on Alston Avenue."

"Oh, I know that church. I go to Gethsemane Baptist."

"That's where Rev. Brown preaches, right?"

"You know Rev. Brown?"

"We are in the Ministerial Association together...."

And so it went with the first few visits. Within the walls of the always dimly lit apartments, there was firm ground on which to stand. Step outside, and the ground seemed to shift. But I was gaining confidence. Two visits, two church-going grandmothers. I could do this.

Then I went to visit Dee. Her three boys were regulars at our house. DeMarcus, Trey and Devon were all within a year of each other, all three quiet, and mischievous. They lived in one of the upstairs apartments of the quadruplex buildings, and as they led me to their apartment, there was visible excitement. Up the steps they ran, fighting to get in front so as to be the first to announce my arrival. Heartened by their exuberance, I sent them in to tell their mom I was there. It became clear immediately that whatever the three boys and I were expecting, it was not what we found in their apartment that afternoon.

"GET THE *HELL* OUT OF THIS HOUSE!" Dee yelled at the boys. "CAN'T YOU SEE I'M TAKING A GOD-DAMNED *NAP*?"

On the little 4'x4' landing at the front door, there was nowhere for me to go. The kids came deflated to the door, yet bravely tried to guard their mother.

"Momma ain't feelin' well today," Trey said to his sneakers.

"Well, maybe another day," I said.

"WHO THE HELL IS AT THAT DOOR?" Dee shouted to her sons.

"That's just Pastor. But he's leaving now, don't worry, Momma."

As the boys tried to soothe their mother's anger, I felt just as helpless and embarrassed as they. I wanted to get off that landing and out of that complex. I had no business intruding on the intimacies of this woman's life. But neither could I simply bail out on the boys. Embarrassed that they had brought me, that momma wasn't welcoming, that I was so awkward, these poor kids had to negotiate some kind of end to this train-wreck of a first encounter. Trying to help, I hollered inside.

"Ms Dee? I'm the pastor up the street. I just wanted to meet the boys' mother. But I can come back another time."

"Aah, *Shit!*" The reply came from inside, but it had a ring of resignation to it and sure enough, a few seconds later the door swung open and there stood Ms Dee, her head peeking around the front door. Her face was puffy and her eyes red and narrow against the outdoor light. She was groggy, as we had awakened her from a long nap. I did not know then that this was her standard condition, the condition of many drug users, I suppose. She stood there waiting for me to say something and all I could think was that I was in way over my head. The only thing that everyone concerned really wanted was a quick out. I told her I was glad to meet her and how nice her boys were. She was shy and suspicious and mumbled thanks. With a quick 'nice to meet you' I headed down the stairs feeling like an idiot. I got her off her couch, having to deal with this strange white man at the door, uninvited, and all I have to say is "nice to meet you."

There are places you know you do not belong. You feel it in your gut that there is nothing for you there but fear and humiliation. The landing to Dee's apartment became such a place for me. I never came to know Dee, really. This first reception was about as good as it got for me. Sometimes it was worse, depending on her condition and whom she had for company. I continued to have her boys hang out with us at our house, and they started coming to church with us eventually. But I could not get over that landing. Everything I had dreaded when I first went into Hearthside was concentrated one flight up on Dee's porch. When I *had* to climb those metal steps, I would do it. But it was never with love in my heart for Dee. It was with fear, and a clear exit strategy.

Good Prayer

Before seminary, I never really knew what to think about prayer. Frankly, I didn't do much praying and when I did, it involved a shopping list of things I wanted from God. When I went to seminary, I still didn't know what to think about prayer. What I did learn, however, was that the shopping list was not the way to go. The real prayer was to pray for God's will to be done. When that got attached to the psychological model of pastoral care into which I was trained, prayer became a vehicle for convincing the sick and ailing that they, too, should accept God's will and thus have their minds soothed. Prayer was to be used to let people know that we should seek God's will, not ours, even in sickness. So to ask for healing, for example, was not only bad theologically, but psychologically, as well. You don't want to give the sick person false hope about being healed. If they are healed, great, but if not, at least they won't have felt let down by God or get too attached to the idea that God would heal them. You can imagine the sophisticated pastoral presence I forged from this learning!

Well, the first time this pastoral presence was requested for prayer for the sick was late one morning, when a group of older folk from our congregation came into the church and invited me to go pray for Rhonda because she had just been diagnosed with cancer. I climbed into the car with them, thinking that this would be an opportunity to demonstrate my pastoral presence. On the way, I was composing the prayer in my head. This was the first time and I wanted to get it right. We arrived and had some conversation until finally someone said, "Pastor, we need to pray." I was ready. So I put my hands on Rhonda's shoulders and prayed. "Lord, we ask you to be with Rhonda in her time of illness."

"Yes, Lord."

So far, so good.

"Be with her as she deals with the news of her cancer."

"Yes, Yes."

"Help her to accept what has come to her and give her peace about her illness. If it is your will, give her healing and health. But if not, let her know your presence. Amen."

In the history of praying, there are no reported cases of someone actually dying because of the prayer that was said over them by their pastor. The good people at Rhonda's house that day must have thought that this might just be the first! They looked at me and then at Rhonda, checking to be sure she was still alive and well. When they were reassured that she had not been put to death by my prayer, they looked once more at me, a mixture of fear and confusion on their faces, wondering what kind of prayer that might be and how the Almighty might respond to such. "Accept her illness"? "*If* it is your will to heal her"? "If *not*"?

Clearly, the unspoken consensus was that such a prayer could only be undone by *real* prayer. The only question was who would be the one to offer the corrective. It fell this day to Cy Johnson. He commenced to praying and I couldn't believe the stuff he said!

"Holy Father, you are the creator of us all. You love us and you hear us when we call to you in need. Rhonda is in need, and we ask you to heal her of this disease. We aren't asking for what you cannot do, Lord. We know you can do what we ask. (He might have added, 'Well, MOST of us know you can!') You healed the blind man so that he could see."

"Yes, Lord!"

"You healed the sick woman when she touched your cloak."

"Yes, you did!"

"You healed my mother when she had cancer...."

"Uh huh!"

"You healed my brother when he had cancer...."

"Yes, Lord!"

"We know that you can do what we ask, and we ask you to touch our sister with your healing spirit, take away all sickness and disease, and restore her to health and wholeness so that she might know the power of your love, the power of your mercy, the power of your healing hand in this very hour!

"We ask this through your beloved Son, the great physician, the healer of us all, Amen!"

"Amen."

Well, really! You can't go praying to God like that! Look at the expectations you raise in a woman such as Rhonda. What if God is not going to heal her? Cy didn't even give that possibility any time in his prayer.

No, he simply prayed as if God were real! As if God actually did the things that the stories of the Bible and of his life said God did.

It was at that time that I began to rethink my understanding of prayer and of God. Cy and the others experienced God in an intimate and openhearted manner and I wanted a part of it. My theological thinking was interesting when I was thinking it, but when I heard that prayer and saw the faith of the people in that room, my psychologically correct prayer was not only faithless and inadequate, it was boring! It treated God as if God were some psychological phantom or immovable, unfeeling force. It would take a long time, and I would have to unlearn a lot before I would be able to pray like Cy. I would have to experience God the way he had.

Even though they had heard me pray, the congregation was still willing to put up a new sign out front to mark my arrival. I was glad for it, because the old one was rotting and barely legible. Will Schuldt was given the task of doing the stone work because he had been doing stone work since stone was invented. He intended to construct a stone wall, some eight feet long and four feet high onto which a painted metal sign would be attached. On a hot and muggy North Carolina summer morning, the men of the congregation gathered around the strong, knowledgeable mason. I wandered out to talk with the guys and watch them work. They had laid out the stones around the cement slab they had poured the week before. Before Will began to lay the stones, they explained to me what was about to take place. They were going to use a running bond, the traditional staggered look you see with most brick or block walls.

"What do you think, Pastor?"

What do you think, Pastor? This is the question that got me into a lot of trouble over the years. I *think* about things. I have opinions about a lot of stuff. I know what I like and what I don't like. So, when somebody asked me for my opinion, I would give it.

I once heard a radio piece on National Public Radio about a group of Evangelical Christians who decided to leave their particular form of Christianity to join the Orthodox Church. They had been in the Orthodox faith for several years at the time of the interview, and they told the story of how one Sunday they were standing together after the service, having a discussion. An old priest walked up to them and asked them what they were talking about. They said they were talking about what they liked and disliked about the Liturgy.

"What you *like* and *dislike* about the liturgy!" the old priest said. "This is the Divine Liturgy. What you *like* and *dislike* could hardly be less relevant!" Then he turned on his heels and walked away.

Yes! There are times in my life when I simply have to hear these words! "What you like and dislike could hardly be less relevant!" When the color of the carpet is being discussed, when someone wants to replace the pews, when the new sign is being decided upon! At these times, people will come right up and ask, "What do you think, Pastor?" and these are the times to say, "What I think could hardly be less relevant!"

But that's *not* what I said when the men asked me about the sign.

What I said was, "I wonder if it would look better stacked."

"Well," somebody said, "we did consider that, but Will thinks we ought to do it this other way."

I was feeling pretty good that my idea was in the realm of possibility, and that gave me some confidence to forge on.

"Have you considered a different pattern?"

At this, a couple guys pushed their hats back on their heads to scratch their foreheads, another got real interested in the mound of dirt at his feet, and there was general hemming and hawing.

The project had run into a snag and the workers needed time to consider their predicament.

'We gave the new pastor an easy one, and he muffed it. We don't want to make him look silly, but we don't want to be out here all day in the sun. How should we proceed?'

Finally Sam, a wise and seasoned man, spoke up.

"Now Pastor, it's gettin' kinda hot out here today, and we've got these men here waiting to get this wall built."

"I know," I said, "but we do want this wall to be right."

At this point, I am sure Will's blood pressure was rising.

Diplomatically, Sam took me aside, lowering his voice.

"Pastor, it is going to be hot today. On top of that, you don't know this, but Will is not a well man. His kidneys are bothering him and we can't keep him out here all day. Now, frankly, the way he wants to do it would be best, and he'd know. I think we ought to let him do the job."

Of course we ought to let him do the job! I knew *nothing* of masonry! What was I doing? Even as Sam returned to the crew, my face grew hot with the dawning realization of just how foolish I was being. I mumbled something I hoped they heard as encouragement, and walked away worrying about what these men thought of me.

It ended up that Will Schuldt, for one, wanted me to know exactly what he thought of me! Three days after the sign fiasco, I got a call from Norma, Will's wife, inviting me over to their house for a visit. I knew I was in trouble, that I had insulted a charter member of the congregation, but there was nothing to be done. I had to accept the invitation and face the music. By the time I arrived at the Schuldt house the next week, I was tied up in knots trying to figure out what I was going to say to defend my ridiculous actions. Will and Norma invited me in, sat me down and we visited for a while. I heard about their kids, most of them grown and on their own, their careers, and their health. Then Norma looked at her husband as if she expected him to take over the conversation. And indeed, he did. Now came the *real* reason for my being there. Will sat at the head of their dining room table and spoke to me calmly, and with great sincerity.

"Pastor, we have been here since the start of Abiding Savior Lutheran Church. God has been good to us. We have seen His hand in our lives, in the people who attend the church and in the pastors, too. We have known all the pastors that have preached at this church. Some have been better preachers, some better pastors, but up to now, we have been supportive of every single one because we know God has blessed us through them."

Up to now! I heard that and realized that I had ruined the streak. Twenty-five years and now the Schuldt family found someone they couldn't tolerate!

"And we want you to know that we support you too. If you or your wife or children need anything, anything at all, all you need to do is come through this door and we will do whatever we can for you. That goes for my boys and for my daughter as well."

My eyes darted back and forth across the kitchen table, from Will to Norma, taking in this astonishing gift and thinking of a possible response. Nothing came, except that I looked this man in the eyes and thanked him.

A few years later I received another call from Norma. This time it was to tell me that Will was heading for the emergency room. I got into my pickup and raced to the hospital, arriving at the same time as Norma and her family. "I think we lost him, Pastor," she said to me in the parking lot. We went in to the hospital together and, sure enough, Will was dead. The emergency room was busy, so the nurse asked me to go in first to see to it that Will's body was presentable for the family. Alone in the room with him, I pondered the strength of this quiet man. I wondered how his family would fare now that he was gone. But when the family came in to see him, I realized that I did not need to worry. Norma and her children gathered around Will and they consoled one another as Norma said, "Pastor, he's gone now. Would you say a prayer?" And because of their influence on me from that very first visit to the Schuldt home and because Cy had demonstrated what prayer to the *living* God was like, I was able say a prayer, a *real* prayer of thanksgiving for a steadfast life. It was a good prayer.

Unwelcome Company

"Don't pull in here, Pastor, park down the road a little ways."

"But the pizzeria is right there."

"Like I said, just go on and park a ways down."

So it was that we ended up parked in front of Sunny's Surf Shop instead of Bud's Pizza and Beer, which I thought had been our destination.

The men of the church were on a fishing trip to the North Carolina coast. We arrived in the evening to spend the night, before being at the dock by 5:00 the next morning. When we arrived at the hotel we were hungry and decided to order out. Several of us piled into the van to pick up the pizza and now we were parked in the lot down the block from Bud's, and I had no idea what was going on.

Don said, "I know a place up the coast, but it's another 25 miles." Somebody else wondered just exactly how hungry people really were. I was listening to the conversation, but I had no idea what they were talking about or why!

It all seemed pretty clear to me. We were there, the pizza was ready and all we had to do was get out of the van, walk across the parking lot and pick it up. Finally I asked, "Why are we not getting pizza here?"

Realizing that the pastor was without a clue, Robert set about explaining.

"Pastor, it's pretty clear that Bud's is not going to be very welcoming to us." I looked over at Bud's. It seemed like your basic pizza and beer joint. I saw nothing unusual about it at all and, frankly, I thought the whole thing was a little silly. "It looks okay to me," I said. "How do you know what it's like inside?"

Robert took a deep breath and said, "Pastor, we are black men. We *have* to know."

Now, at least, I knew what the problem was. Or so I thought. The problem was that these men could not go into Bud's to pick up the pizza because of their race. The obvious solution to that was to send me in to do it.

"Y'all remember. I used to hang wallpaper for a living. I probably *know* some of these guys. Why don't I just go get the pizza?"

It seemed like a logical thing to do. But it did not catch on at first. It was as if nobody had heard me. Strange, I thought. The solution to the problem was so obvious, and yet nobody was seeing it.

Here's the thing. I finally did, after much debate, get sent into Bud's to pick up the pizzas. But of course, that was never the problem. The problem was that African-American men still had to know what places would accept them and which would not. The problem was that these men had a pastor with no insight into their reality. The problem was that this pastor's proposed solution to the false problem left these men-- great men, including Civil Rights activists who marched with Martin Luther King, Jr., pioneers who were some of the first African-Americans to cross the color barrier at major universities in the South and a member of the famed Tuskegee Airmen--it left these history making men sitting out in the van.

Meanwhile, their pastor, thinking only of getting some pizza, walked obliviously across the parking lot. All I thought was that I had solved our problem. I *was* the problem. Everybody knew it but me. Still, as I walked, I heard Don call from behind me. I turned to see him jogging to catch up.

"Pastor, we just can't let you go in there alone."

"Well, then, are you coming in with me or are we going somewhere else?"

"No, I'm coming in with you."

And so we entered Bud's and sure enough, it was a honky-tonk. 'How did they know?' I wondered. I can only imagine what Don was thinking, but he seemed to be calm enough. I went to get the pizzas and, of course, they weren't ready yet, so I asked Don if he thought we ought to order a beer. "No," he said, "We ought to sit at the table nearest the door and wait." So we did.

With country music playing and good ol' boys drinking, that wait took a long, long time.

Nobody approached us, nobody hassled us. We just sat by the door and waited. What I most remember was the growing sense of resentment inside me. I resented feeling scared of the potential trouble that might arise. I could have gone into that bar without a second thought to my status. But in this particular situation, I had to lay low and try not to draw attention to us. Truth to tell, I was way more put out by my having to cower than I was at the fact that someone like Don, a doctor of dentistry and respected man in the community had to do so time and time again. And now, he had to put himself in that situation one more time because he had to watch the back of his white pastor! At the time, though, all I was thinking was, 'if only he would have stayed in the van, we wouldn't be in this mess.'

Lord, have mercy.

Here was an African-American man intentionally putting aside his safety (again!), to enter into a place where he was not going to be respected (again!), in order to accompany me. My response was to blame him for "creating" the problem. I didn't think I needed accompaniment and would have preferred to be left alone. I had a free pass into Bud's. 'Let me go inside and take care of it!'

But they didn't leave me alone. On one level, Don came with me because I might need support. It is humbling to realize that while I was making no connection to the plight of these men, they were making the connection for me. Concerning the honky-tonk, they seemed to think, 'If it's bad for us, it's bad for him', so they sent someone to accompany me. On another level, though, his accompaniment was not about my safety, but my initiation. If I was to be pastor to these men, I had to know something about their reality. Not just know it, but experience it. No free passes. I may not have wanted to be in solidarity with them at that moment, but they were perfectly clear. "We are in this together, Pastor."

Small Things

St. Bonaventure said, "A constant fidelity in small things is a great and heroic virtue."

Yeah, right.

By 33, Martin Luther King Jr. had won the Nobel Peace Prize. Me? At 33, I was still wondering what I was going to be when I grew up. I knew it was going to be more than being a *pastor*. Where was the excitement in a local church? Where was the inspiration? What was the great cause into which I was to be thrust? I remember thinking, 'This cannot be all I am for!'

I was reminded of that early crisis recently. My daughter Rosa had the good fortune of spending a day with John Prendergast, the human rights activist who has brought international attention to Darfur and the horrors of the Sudan. Rosa was elated and inspired. And of course, I had occasion to take stock once more.

"Let's see, John Prendergast goes to Darfur to witness and write about the horrible genocide there. I go watch the women make quilts to send to Darfur. He raises millions of dollars to re-settle victims of war. I go to a council meeting to talk about being behind in the church budget. This cannot be all I am for!"

But what if St. Bonaventure was right? What if faithfully showing up in small, insignificant ways turns into something great and heroic? In the past twenty-five years, anyone who has stuck around has seen great trends and historic movements come right to his or her front door.

Rebecca Davis came to mine. A member of the church and nurse at the hospital, she was looking for someone with some Spanish to accompany a family through their visits to the pediatric HIV clinic at Duke University Medical Center. Of course, I knew about HIV and AIDS and had tried to educate myself about it, especially in light of the blaming and condemning that came from some Christian quarters. But I was not *involved* in it. I was preaching and teaching, doing evangelism, and working with the kids in the youth program.

Translators at the hospital were at a premium, however, and could not be tied up all day with one patient. Rebecca urged me to call the clinic. She had the phone number ready.

I called and spoke with the social worker in charge of the volunteer program. She seemed to have been expecting my call. I thought for a second about Rebecca and her readiness with the phone number. Sure enough, within the week, I was being oriented to the program as a volunteer. Each volunteer was assigned a specific patient, to assure consistency for the children. I was assigned to Alicia, nine years old and her grandmother, Maria-Carmen. The first day we met, several things surprised me. The first was Alicia's energy. She talked a mile a minute, asking questions and making observations far faster than my feeble Spanish could keep up. She was at the HIV clinic and had AIDS, yet acted as if she had the world by the tail.

The second thing that surprised me was how very thin she was, a skeleton with skin, really. Maria-Carmen, by contrast, was short and plump, barely uttering a word, and grave in her demeanor. She had gone down this long, slow road with her daughter, who had died two years earlier. Now accompanying her granddaughter, Maria-Carmen was stoic and cautious.

She and I sat quietly and spoke of the medical realities of her granddaughter, the difficulties of having a young girl with AIDS who was unwanted at school and lonely at home. By contrast, Alicia always wanted to be playing and moving. She loved going to the various offices and labs, anything to keep from sitting still. When there was time, she would head straight to the play area that the hospital had provided for the kids. It was one of the only places where Alicia could play with others without drawing scorn from other kids' parents.

Over the course of two years, I hung out with Alicia once every two months. In those days, the people who worked in the clinic were lamps of hope to the kids and parents who came in, but a clandestine lamp. The pall of AIDS was still so strong that people sometimes snuck into the AIDS clinic, not wanting to be seen there. Even hearing that I volunteered there made some people nervous.

"Join the club," I would say, thinking about the last time I was in the playroom, snotty-nosed kids using me for a jungle-gym. In those days, fear was high, and I was not immune.

The more time spent at the clinic, however, the easier it became. Alicia continued her visits, her *abuela* faithfully attending with her. Inevitably, Alicia was getting more severely ill. Her energy waned as every little cold turned into more serious respiratory illness. By the end, that uncontrollable bundle of energy was constrained to an oxygen tank and a hospital bed. No more visits to the playroom, no need to chase after her or entertain her. There was no more energy to contain. She died with her *abuela* with her.

My role in the clinic continued. One wing of the children's hospital was dedicated to AIDS babies and small children. I began to visit that wing and found, true to form of most hospitals, the staff was overloaded. The very first day on the wing, I wandered into the room of a little baby girl who was born with AIDS. She cried constantly for the horrible stomach pain and diaper rash that came with chronic diarrhea. The nurse gave me a quick introduction to the room: how to take the crib down to get to the baby, how the

IV was hooked up, how to hold the child without getting tangled in the tubes. There was a beautiful rocking chair to sit in, television if I wanted it. Then she was out the door to take care of her other patients.

"What is the baby's name?" I asked as she was leaving.

"Michelle. We named her Michelle."

"We named her? What do you mean, we named her?"

"She came in orphaned, so we named her. Beautiful, isn't she?" And off she went.

As it happened, Baby Michelle was three months old, the same age as our baby Rosa at home. The contrast of their lives would be an ongoing source of wonder and sadness to me. But just then, I was eager to get to know Michelle in that hospital room. She was lying in her metal-cage-of-a-crib, crying. I let down the side panel, fetched her out and settled in with her on the rocking chair. I have a lousy singing voice, but infants don't seem to mind. So I sang to her as we rocked. In no time at all, she was quiet and nestled into my chest as I sang Taize chants into her little ears. I was thinking about this child in my arms, suffering an illness that not only left her sick and dying, but abandoned, as well. She should have been fussed over and admired, not put away from the world. And I thought about the world that was so frightened by this illness and how foreboding was this room and hospital wing. And, of course, I thought about my own little baby at home and was very thankful for her good health and joy.

Then Michelle started to squirm. I changed her position, but it didn't help. I tried another, but, again, no help. I stood up to walk with her, trying to get her comfortable once more, when there came an awful explosion of diarrhea! It came through her diaper and onto my hands, arms and shirt. It was everywhere! Now, I have had babies poop on me before, so I didn't panic. I set her down safely in the crib and pulled up the metal panel. I noticed that Michelle had stopped fussing for the time being, so I started to get myself washed off. Before I got too far along on that, however, Michelle began to complain again, this time, I figured, from the discomfort of the dirty diaper. So I finished getting cleaned up and wandered out to the hallway to let the nurse know that the baby needed changing. I went to the nurse's station. Nobody. I went down the hall. Nobody. I went all around the wing until I found the nurse who had introduced me to Michelle and told her that the baby needed some attention.

She said, "I will get to her just as soon as I can, but I have two or three ahead of her. If you want, you can change her. Just be very gentle with her bottom and use the Desitin. It's in the room on the shelf. Oh, and use gloves."

'Well, it's a little late for that!' I thought.

So I went back to the room, got the wipes and the diaper, the changing cloth and the ointment. I took that baby out of her crib again, laid her down on the changing table and set about the task. It was just like changing every other diaper I had ever changed, save for two things. The first was that when I cleaned off this little baby's behind, I nearly wept to see the rawness of her skin. Blood and pus mingled with the diarrhea. All I could do was dab her clean as gently as possible, apologizing the whole time.

The second was that I had never before felt threatened by changing a diaper. But this time, I did. What could I be picking up by handling this child's mess? And again, I thought of my own daughter. What could I be picking up that she might catch? Finally, though, here was this baby who needed tending to, and no one else was available. It was the most grisly, the most frightening and the most prayerful diaper change of my career.

What Am I For?

Darla was a retired schoolteacher who moved to Durham from the D.C. area to be closer to her grandchildren. She was a quiet woman. On first encounter, you would think her incapable of controlling a classroom full of elementary school kids. Too quiet to be heard, you might think. But spend any time at all with her and you realized that you were quieting down, too. You realized that you were holding your tongue, not wanting to say just anything. You realized that she would control her classroom just fine, thank you very much, simply with her dignity. She would look you straight in the eyes, listen attentively and thoughtfully, answer with an economy of words and leave you feeling like you wanted to stay in her company and in her good graces.

Darla asked me to come visit her one afternoon and she met me at the door. She invited me in and on the landing just inside the door she said to me, "Now, be careful of the step. Oh, I don't need to tell you that. You have been here before; *you* remember these things."

I thought that was a little strange, but gave it no more thought until after we had sat down to talk. As usual, Darla was gracious, but she had something on her mind. It ends up she had just been diagnosed with Alzheimer's. It was in the early stages, she explained, but she could notice that she was forgetting things and was fearful of all that might come from the disease. For Darla to be facing a loss of her dignity was a sad thought. But she gave me a great gift. She invited me to walk with her on the journey. She wanted to talk and to pray through her ordeal. She looked to me as her pastor to be the one to do that with. So over two years, I was given the wonderful gift of walking with Darla into Alzheimer's. She wanted me to understand what was going on inside her mind so that I could continue to talk with her. Thoughts were clear, she said, but she couldn't get them to her mouth. She noticed that it got more difficult to speak when she was upset, sad or angry. I was able to get a sense of what the process of forgetfulness was like for her. I think she truly appreciated that I was willing to go there with her and I surely was blessed to be attending to this process with her.

As time went on, Darla began to lose her train of thought in mid-sentence. She would stop and apologize. It got to where she did not want to speak, though she still had much to say, so we made an agreement. I told her that I would be a very careful listener and if she lost her train of thought, I would prompt her with what she had been saying. For some months, this was a very effective way of keeping her mind on track. She would pick up where she had gotten lost and keep on going. After a while, however, she got less and less able to do that, and felt greater pressure to try to remember, which, of course, made it harder for her to remember. We made a new agreement that if she did forget, and my prompting didn't help, we would laugh and go on with something else. That seemed to take some of the pressure off her, making it easier for her to remember.

Her husband, busying himself in the kitchen, looked at us like we were children misbehaving whenever we joked about faulty memory. He looked at us with his head shaking and hands on his hips. Then he'd smile. It was a great blessing that he understood that Darla needed someone with whom to talk and to laugh. He, poor guy, was the caretaker. His job was not nearly as fun or as casual as mine. For him, the daily chores of bathing, dressing and feeding Darla were relentless. Still, he supported our relationship.

One of the most important things we did together over the years, as her Alzheimer's continued to deteriorate, was to say the Lord's Prayer together. On days when she had a hard time remembering much of anything, she could still recite the Lord's Prayer. Each time she did, I would point out to her that she remembered the prayer and she would always straighten up and say, "I did, didn't I?"

I noticed that Darla would not speak much if there were other people in the room with us. She was keenly aware of our agreements, but had no such agreements with others, so she kept her thoughts to herself. Most of what Darla got from her family and friends was the important day-to-day buoying and encouragement that she truly did need in order to keep going. But with her pastor, she did talk of fear and mortality. On one such occasion, as Darla was slipping further into depression and weakness, I asked her if she thought that she was dying. She said that she thought she might be. "Are you too tired to keep going?" I asked. She said that she needed to for her husband and her children. And what did she need, I wondered?

"Oh, to rest."

In the course of this conversation, Darla's son, who lived up north and had come to visit his mother, slipped into the doorway of the room and listened in. I later found out that he was furious at me for having such a conversation with his mother. Of course, he had no way of knowing that she and I talked like this all the time. He saw this exchange as very negative in a time his mother needed positive energy to heal and he was being protective. Interestingly, I never had to deal with him about this, because his father and sister explained to him their understanding of pastoral ministry. And their explanation was as concise and accurate as any theologian's. "Now, he's the pastor. He is supposed to talk with people about life and death. He's the one we called to tell us the truth, even if we don't want to hear it. He isn't making this up. He's just letting Darla talk about the truth. She needs someone who will do that. Don't get mad. He's doing his job."

My job: to visit a woman who by the end of the day wouldn't even remember that I had been there. To accompany a little girl who would never make it into fourth grade. To tend a baby who would never make it out of infancy, to visit the sick and elderly, to lead a small group of people in worship and prayer. Does faithfulness in these small things make for a great and heroic life? All I know is that this *is* what I am for.

Nowhere to Hide

"Pastor, would you be willing to say a few words at my mother's funeral?"

"Of course I would, Rebecca. I'd be honored."

"Well, I'd understand if you don't want to. You won't be welcomed over there."

"It'll be fine, Rebecca."

Famous last words.

The funeral in question was to be held at the Greater Heavenly Glory Church, the Reverend L.D. Johnson, Pastor. I had never been inside this church, but everybody knew that Reverend Johnson was the man in control. Those outside the church wondered how anyone would want to be a part of Greater Heavenly Glory Church, but the membership continued to grow and the people tithed their money and their devotion to Reverend Johnson. He demanded nothing less. Still, this was a funeral: a funeral of one of that church's elderly members. What could be so difficult?

I arrived at the church and was escorted down the narrow hall to Rev. Johnson's office. The doors swung open and I entered into the company of Rev. Johnson's pastors-in-training. There were eight of them seated in front of the grand desk that was obviously the good Reverend's place. Each of the associates rose to greet me as I entered. I knew two of them from the neighborhood and greeted them by name. It seemed that a hint of embarrassment flashed on their faces...or was I being paranoid?

One of the associate pastors ushered me to the one empty seat in front of the looming desk. I sat down, only to realize that my chair was significantly shorter than the others. My eyes barely made it over the desk next to which I was sitting. I was a school kid in trouble in the principal's office! I knew this was a game of one-upmanship and I did not want to enter into it. Seated at the little chair, I fought off the feelings of insecurity, reminding myself that I was a mature adult and an experienced pastor. There was no need for anxiety or resentment, so I should calm down. That these feelings rose up in me right away indicated that maybe I was not as mature as I thought!

That could have started a downward spiral, but that's as far as I got before Rev. Johnson made his entrance. He came in from the back of the office so that he greeted everyone from behind the office desk. I stood to greet him, extending my hand across the desk and introducing myself. He shook my hand without a word and gestured for me to sit down.

Addressing his remarks to his associate pastors, he explained the service and assigned roles for each. I was given a time to 'bring a few words' towards the end of the program. Then we gathered together for our entrance and into the chancel we went. It is traditional in the South in many churches that the preachers all sit behind the pulpit, which is the focal point of the sanctuary. I took my seat behind the pulpit and the service began. There were hundreds of people there as Rebecca's mother was much beloved. Through the eulogies and the greetings everything went beautifully.

Then Rev. Johnson stood to preach. He began in the enticingly slow, deliberate manner of one who knew he had something to say to a people dying to hear it, but who knew they could not bear it all at once. People leaned in, eager for the word. Gradually, the pace picked up and the preaching began in earnest, the style eloquent and electrifying.

Content, however, was another matter. For, while he was preaching at the funeral of one of his long time members, he barely acknowledged the fact of her death. It was as if her death were a personal insult to him. Of course, *she* could not be chastised for dying, so the good Reverend took to condemning others: a host of people deserving the fires of hell, and taking his time with each! Beginning with "abortionists," he made his way through gays and lesbians, "so-called" Christians, and people on welfare. The insult of death was so deep and personal, the response went on for nearly an hour. It was an entirely inappropriate sermon on many levels, but Rev. Johnson went the extra mile just for me. As he condemned each of the offending groups, he would wait until just the right time to turn to look at me.

"...These abortionists killing babies! And the church"--his back to the congregation, his arm reaching out to point an accusing finger straight at me--"not saying one word about it!"

"Men too lazy to work for a living, and pastors"--his arm extending behind him, pointing straight at me--"encouraging them to be slothful!"

With each new group of "sinners," I was handed a membership card. Of course, there was nothing I could do but wait it out.

'This is his show,' I kept reminding myself.

'You were warned,' I repeated. All the while, my resentment grew and I tried to formulate a response that I could use when it was my turn to speak. Of course, it couldn't *sound* like a response. It had to be subtle, understated. There would be no direct rebuttal, but something that would let everyone know exactly what I thought about this sermon and its messenger.

"Men loving men. And fool preachers"--turning, looking straight at me, raised arm, pause for emphasis--"fool preachers standing up there doing their wedding ceremonies!"

Sitting in the chair in front of the entire congregation, perfectly stationed to be the visual aid for the sermon, there was no place to hide and no way to defend myself.

Then it dawned on me. 'There is no place to hide and no way to defend myself!' At this, a profound calm came over me. The resentment vanished; I let go of trying to think of a response. As Rev. Johnson found more and more creative ways to make it clear that I was not appreciated on his pulpit, his scorn no longer made the least bit of difference to me. In fact, I found myself laughing at the disparaging remarks he made at my expense.

It's strange how being utterly defenseless can be so empowering. The whole scene began to turn. The harder Reverend Johnson tried to humiliate me, the more it became clear that he was working way too hard. He continued on his tirade, but it no longer held sway.

When the sermon was over, it was my turn at the pulpit. Every retort I had thought about and every desire to dig back at Rev. Johnson dissolved away in that moment. It was clear what the family and congregation needed. Stepping up to the pulpit, I said, "In this time of loss and sorrow, let us turn to the God of comfort as we recite together the 23rd Psalm.

"The Lord is my Shepherd, I shall not be in want. He makes me to lie down in green pastures and leads me beside the still waters. He restores my soul and leads me in the path of righteousness for His name's sake. Yea, though I walk through the valley of the shadow of death, I will fear no evil...."

Years later, I had a dream. I found myself in a prison cell, the guard handing me an orange jumpsuit.

"Put it on," he said. Shaken and in a panic, I couldn't even unbutton my shirt to get undressed. What was I in prison for? Did my family know where I was? Could I get word to them? How could this be happening? Then, in an instant, it dawned on me that there was not a thing I could do to get word to anyone. Whatever was to happen, there was nothing to be done about it. I calmly unbuttoned my shirt and put on prison garb.

Then I was escorted down a narrow hallway and put into another uncomfortable seat: the electric chair. Taking my seat, I listened to the prosecuting attorney as he recapped the trial for four or five people sitting before me to watch my execution. As he went on, it became clear that I had been tried as an accomplice to a violent crime. The people waiting to watch me die were the family of the victim, but when they heard I was not the actual perpetrator, they were surprised and disappointed. The attorney said that I was an accomplice to the crime and that I was found guilty. Someone asked why I was getting the death penalty and the attorney answered, "Because he did not have a lawyer!"

"It doesn't matter. He was tried, found guilty and it's too late to change it." Then a helmet was put on my head, which I calmly received, resigned to my impending death. The order was given to throw the switch, and...nothing happened! No electricity, no execution, nothing. The system failed. The attorney then said, "We cannot execute him twice, so I guess he is free to go!" Next thing I knew, I was standing outside the prison walls, feeling completely calm and profoundly free.

'Whoa,' I thought, reveling, '*this* is what Jesus means about losing your life to gain it.'

The Turkey Wars

As the director of the local food bank, I experience the pressure to live up to expectations, even conflicting ones. For two hours every Tuesday morning, over a hundred clients flood our match-box sized building to receive forty to fifty pounds of dry goods, produce, meat and canned goods. At Thanksgiving and Christmas time, the number jumps to close to two hundred people and we give away turkeys and hams bought by the generous donations of community members.

My sense is that I am a flexible, kind and generous person at the food bank. I also feel that I am just and wise about making decisions based on the unique circumstances of our clients. Most weeks of the year, people can pick up food for friends and relatives who couldn't get there for one reason or another. No problem. During the holiday, they can do the same thing. The only difference is that you don't get a ham or turkey if you are not there to pick it up. We limit it to one per customer until every client who has shown up gets one. Then, just before we close for the day, people can check back to see if there are extras. If so, they may take one for their absent friends. But before then, it is one per customer. After all these years, I still have to hear how unfair I am being, how untrusting and un-Christian I am to not let people take a turkey for their friends or family right now!

I swallow hard and hold to the rule. I also feel the knot in my stomach as I am accused of being unyielding and un-Christian, as if I were letting Jesus down by not letting people get everything they want. Rather than the holidays being joyful, they sometimes leave me torn and dissatisfied with myself. What if they are right? What if the policy is unreasonable? What if people think I am a jerk? This is the spirit of fear, fear of being seen as less than what I think I am supposed to be. Call it chronic anxiety. It is this subtle spirit of fear that drives me to maintain my identity as a more faithful Christian, a just community servant, a nice guy. Of course, in this scenario, I cannot be both a nice guy and a just person. Either I give in to the wants of everyone, or I hold out for the last in line. I choose one and feel inadequate for the other. I can't win!

So here we were at Christmas again. I told myself that I was not going to let these people get to me this year. I was going to cheerfully explain the policy and maintain the Christmas spirit. The first few who confronted me got the policy explained to them in true Christmas spirit. I listened to them patiently as they complained and accused. I apologized for inconveniencing them and kept helping people through the line. A couple more complained and I politely explained the policy...again.

About a half hour in, another woman came through the line, found me in the chaos and gave it to me with both barrels. "This is not fair to people who cannot be here! You are not being Christian!" I was just about to explain the policy in true Christmas spirit, one more *stinking* time, when she added, "You know, you are being a real asshole about this!"

That was it!

"You know, you are absolutely right!" I said, as I stood up on my chair.

"Can I have your attention, please?" I yelled in the midst of the room full of the energy of the holiday season.

"Please quiet down!" I continued. "I do not care if you have been picking up for the same people for fifteen years. I do not care if you feel horrible that you cannot get them a turkey or a ham today. But nobody is leaving this building with more than one ham or turkey! I mean nobody! Today I am an equal opportunity asshole!"

Everybody busted out laughing. The volunteers shouted, "It's true, he has been an asshole to everybody all morning!" Even the lady who had been giving me a hard time laughed and relented.

I don't know what I thought would happen if I didn't live up to all my standards. I must have thought it would be something horrible. But when everybody knew what I had tried to hide and maneuver around, the shame that I had bottled up inside of me dissipated completely. What an exquisite surprise to find release and joy!

Joy and freedom; this is the way I want to live and the way to this life is not by avoiding committing stupid, insensitive, unkind acts. The key for me is to let people in on the internal struggle, to not be taken in by the temptation to hide my shame or my imperfection. Freedom comes with letting people in and laying down my defenses. I stumbled onto this simple insight at the food bank that day and it made me want to try it again!

The opportunity came quickly, as it always does when we are talking about our desire to defend ourselves. A member of my congregation came down to the sermon discussion group after the service on Sunday, angry and upset about some "half-truth" I had spoken, with which he took offense. A typical response from me would have been to feel anxious, look for a way to justify my position, get him to understand what I meant to say. I resisted all of these as I sat in the circle opposite him and listened intently to what he had to say.

It ends up that little he railed about had to do with what I had said. Other pressing issues in his life poured out. His words might not have made any sense, but because I was listening with an open heart, I heard the deeper pain and struggle of a hurting man. Without the distraction of defending myself, it was effortless.

Bringing It Home

Practicing vulnerability in ministry has brought me to a most difficult and threatening place, my own household. That is where I have the hardest time letting go. There are times when I cannot figure out what it is I am supposed to let go of! An Italian by birth and rearing, my parenting style is a mix of fierce love, pride and delight, and the occasional out of the blue expression of paternal authoritarianism! My wife has always tried to get me to understand the dynamics involved. It happens something like this: I will get frustrated or tired and put my foot down on a topic. Later, my wife will tell me that I shut the children out by doing so and make them feel they have no voice. To me, this feels like she is placing herself as the mediator between our children and me. Knowing that I have a good relationship with them, I resist mightily the insinuation that I was not respecting our children's feelings. This played itself out for years and was the most difficult part of an otherwise wonderful relationship between my wife and me.

A short time after the food bank incident, we entered again into the mire. My wife Virginia knew it was coming, as she always does, and I did not. But suddenly, it seemed, I was getting irritated responses to my questions from my daughters, who had been friendly only minutes before. I then got irritated back, and my wife sighed. It was happening again. "Why are you getting irritated?" I asked my daughter, Emma.

"Because you are," my wife shot at me.

"NO, I am NOT!"

"Yes, you are, Daddy," came the choir from the back seat.

My ego took the hit and I got angry, then quiet and then withdrawn; that familiar dynamic of shame.

Three days later, I was still not really communicating with Virginia. I was mad, embarrassed, had my pride hurt. Okay, I was sulking. What was different, though, was that now I had a clue about how to approach the problem. I began to try to sort out what I was trying to defend, but what it was did not show itself readily. "What needs to die?" was the constant question, but there was no response. Finally, that third night, I at least needed to tell Virginia that I was working on understanding my part in this mess. I told Virginia that I was trying to figure out what I was trying to defend, but had not figured out what. Was it an image of being a good father, of being a good communicator with my kids, of being the head of the household, something? But they were not quite it.

Virginia reassured me that I was a great father, that she did not want me to feel bad about my relationship with the kids.

"That is not the issue, though." I tried to explain. "There has got to be something here that I am holding onto, that I am supposed to let go."

"Well, if this is something between you and God, I am going to bow out, because I can't help you there!"

"Fair enough," I said, and rolled over to go to sleep.

But then it came to me.

"Submit to her."

Now, while I sometimes lapse into wanting others to submit to me, generally I'm as egalitarian as the next guy. Submission is not a quality I have nurtured in myself or in others. Therefore, my response to this clear word was, "I'm sorry. What was that?"

"Submit to her."

"Dang!"

"Are you still awake?" I asked Virginia.

"Of course I am." she replied.

"Well, I think it has come to me. I am supposed to submit to you. What do you think about that?"

There was a moment of silence. Maybe she was stunned to hear such a thing from me. But no, she was simply gathering her thoughts.

"That might be good. Then I would not have to choose between sticking up for the kids and risking hurting your feelings. We could actually talk about things openly and honestly. It would mean we could avoid these times of alienation. It would mean…."

"Yeah, I think I get it." I laughed.

And I had gotten it. Her understanding of my relationship with the kids was accurate. My letting go meant that it was time to hearken to her understanding. I knew it was right and true the moment the words had come to me. The shame, the hurt, the pit in my stomach had disappeared in an instant, leaving me free to love my children and my wife differently, more gently.

Three days of alienation and struggle, though! I had hoped that my newfound insight would yield fruit a little more quickly than that! But then, three days is our story, isn't it?

Epilogue

It's been months now since the stories in this book were gathered. The process of writing has helped me better notice when my defenses go up. I remind myself that there is no need to defend anything. I laugh when I find myself falling back into my old patterns. Good thing, too, because the instinct to defend myself is still really strong. Just the other day our family was out to dinner. We were walking back to the car, when out of the bookstore came Chuck. Chuck is a local character with poor health and a drinking problem. He and I have been friends for years. This night, though, when we encountered him, he was not himself.

I said, "Chuck! How's it going? Haven't seen you in a long time."

"Yeah."

I said, "Well, how's it going?"

"Huh."

This wasn't like Chuck. I knew something isn't right.

He said, "Whoa, huh. I'm not very happy with you."

"Chuck, what's the matter?" I said.

"I thought you were going to visit me in the hospital."

Visit you in the hospital?? Shit, Chuck. You called me from Wenatchee to tell me you were in the hospital there. That's when I told you I would visit you. Wenatchee is an hour away. Then you called the next day and you were in Moses Lake, that's like two and a half hours away. I didn't have time to schlep all the way from here to Moses Lake to see you, man! I have been slammed these last three weeks; funerals, pastoral obligations, negotiations with the city for a new location for the food bank. I just couldn't get there! Hell, you're not even a member of our congregation!

Not even a member? Where did that come from?

All I can say is that this response was in place and ready to go before Chuck had even finished talking. Scary how fast it happens and shameful how petty it can be.

The good news, this time, is that I did not say any of it out loud. As quickly as it came, there also came the reminder, "You are dead, let it go."

So I did let it go…a little.

"I did say that, didn't I?"

"Yeah. Huh. You didn't come. You're a man of God. You're supposed to give people hope and support."

Yeah, but….

"People need a little hope in their lives, ya know? When you say you're going to visit somebody, you should do it."

Yeah, but….

"Since I've known you, I've looked up to you, but I was real disappointed you didn't come to see me."

Yeah, but….

Let it all go!

"You're right, man. I said I was going to visit you, and I didn't do it. I'm really sorry and I hope you can forgive me."

At this, Chuck smiles and says, "Aw, I already forgot about it. Now, get the hell outta here. Your family's waitin'."

And he gives me a little push. It feels like a nudge toward freedom.

Made in the USA
Charleston, SC
09 October 2013